New

BIBLE READINGS FOR SPECIAL TIMES

...for those times when we want to hear God's word speaking to us clearly

Lindsay Melluish

Published by
The Bible Reading Fellowship
First Floor, Elsfield Hall
15–17 Elsfield Way, Oxford OX2 8FG

ISBN-10 1 84101 487 7
ISBN-13 978 1 84101 487 6

First published 2006
10 9 8 7 6 5 4 3 2 1 0

Acknowledgments
Scripture quotations are taken from the Holy Bible, New International Version, copyright © 1973, 1978, 1984 by International Bible Society, are used by permission of Hodder & Stoughton Limited. All rights reserved. 'NIV' is a registered trademark of International Bible Society. UK trademark number 1448790.

A catalogue record for this book is available from the British Library

Printed by Gutenberg Press, Tarxien, Malta

Introduction

Welcome to parenthood! You have just begun one of the most exciting adventures of your life. However much people might be warning you about the terrible twos or the dreaded teens, you don't need to take too much notice!

Of course, every adventure has its fair share of scary moments and challenges—it might even be that those are outweighing the excitement just now, for whatever reason. Maybe the pregnancy was unplanned and you're still coming to terms with it all, or perhaps the whole adjustment of caring for a baby feels daunting. But it is very likely that any feelings like that will soon pass and you can look forward to lots of fun, some great achievements along the way and some moments of sheer delight at the whole experience.

I began this adventure, along with my husband Mark, just 17 years ago when I became pregnant with our first child. We now have five children, aged 17 down to 6, two girls and three boys. During this time we have had our fair share of highs and lows, including a long period of infertility when we wondered whether we would be able to have any more children. It hasn't always been easy but we are very thankful to God for our children and for the immense pleasure that they give us.

Perhaps you are reading this because you (or your wife) have recently given birth to a baby for the first time, the second or the third. Perhaps you have recently adopted a child or have just become a foster parent. You might be a married person, knowing the support of a loyal partner. Or you may not. You may be a single parent, dependent on the support of friends and family. Or perhaps you don't have much support at all.

Equally, as you look back on the circumstances of the birth you might be feeling very satisfied with how it all went, or perhaps you feel disappointed with some aspect of it. It might even have left you feeling somewhat shocked or traumatized, especially if there were some kind of complications with the delivery.

Whatever your situation, I pray you will find something in

these readings for you as you care for your new baby. Some of what you will find here may not apply directly to you, but I hope very much that you will allow God to speak through the passages into your unique situation. This is a very special time for you, and he will have so much he wants to say to you right now as you spend even a bit of time with him. He delights in your little one as much as you do—even more so, in fact—and he is extremely interested in helping you as you begin life as a parent.

Just a few final things. Firstly, if you are married and living together with your partner, you might like to follow these readings through together as a couple. If you can carve out time to read and pray together, you will have a firm foundation from which to start.

Next, since I don't know whether you have a boy or a girl, I have tended to alternate when referring to your baby. I hope you won't find this too off-putting, but I felt it was the only way to play fair.

Finally and very importantly, as you begin to read, you will find that these studies are set out to cover a four-week period with a reading for five days in a week and a few verses for the weekend. Let me give you a health warning: don't feel you have to follow it like that! As a new parent, it is quite likely that you will find it difficult to do anything as regularly as you did before the baby was born. Be reassured—it will all settle down again quite soon, and then if you can make it a priority to take a bit of time out each day to be with God, it will really benefit you. But for now, just take the time when you can.

May God bless you as you invite him into your family life, and may you find great riches as you dig into his word for encouragement and guidance.

Quotations are taken from the New International Version of the Bible.

MONDAY

1 SAMUEL 1:26–28a

Thankfulness

[Hannah] said to [Eli], 'As surely as you live, my lord, I am the woman who stood here beside you praying to the Lord. I prayed for this child, and the Lord has granted me what I asked of him. So now I give him to the Lord. For his whole life he will be given over to the Lord.'

Having a new baby is one of the most life-changing events in anyone's experience, and you can feel as though you're the only person in the world who has ever been through anything quite so momentous! It brings up many different emotions, some that we've anticipated in advance, and others which might come more as a surprise. Hannah was no different and, after years of longing for a baby, the overriding emotion that she seems to experience is one of thankfulness. Now, the Lord having granted her request, she expresses her gratitude by taking Samuel and giving him over to God for his whole life.

The Bible encourages thankfulness. Paul says in 1 Thessalonians 5:18 that it is God's will for us. As you ponder the arrival of your new baby, there will almost certainly be so much to give thanks for. So enjoy entering into thankfulness for your precious baby, for a safe delivery, for your own health, for caring hospital staff, for people who have supported you and so on. Even if things didn't go so well, try to give thanks for what was good—it will help speed up the healing process.

Why not make a list of all the things you are thankful for and spend time, either alone or with your partner, thanking God for these things. Like Hannah, you might want to offer your baby's life back to God, and if so, you could arrange to take him to church for a service of thanksgiving and dedication.

'Give thanks to him and praise his name!' (Psalm 100:4).

TUESDAY

GENESIS 21:2, 6–7

Amazement

Sarah became pregnant and bore a son to Abraham in his old age, at the very time God had promised him... Sarah said, 'God has brought me laughter, and everyone who hears about this will laugh with me.' And she added, 'Who would have said to Abraham that Sarah would nurse children? Yet I have borne him a son in his old age.'

Having initially laughed at God's promise of a son for Abraham and Sarah in their old age (Genesis 18:12), Sarah is now understandably astounded at the arrival of her baby. Now she is laughing once again, not out of cynicism this time, but because of her sheer joy and amazement.

In the Christian life, it can be easy to lose that sense of wonder at what God can do. In the busyness of everyday life, we can cease to believe in miracles. Or maybe we have never believed in the first place. But having a baby is often when that sense of wonder comes alive or returns. Whether this is your first or your sixth child, you will doubtless be marvelling at how small she is, at her tiny little fingers and toes, at the fact that she's been inside you all this time and that now you've finally come face to face—and, perhaps most of all, at the fact that God used you and your partner to produce this miracle.

If, like Sarah, you experienced difficulty in conceiving your baby and had medical complications that made having a baby more problematic for you than for others, you may be feeling even more amazed at what God has done.

As you care for your baby today, I encourage you to go with those feelings of amazement and to use them to remind yourself, over and over, of the wonder of God and of his incredible power.

'Stop and consider God's wonders!' (Job 37:14).

WEDNESDAY

GENESIS 25:21–22

Confusion

Isaac prayed to the Lord on behalf of his wife, because she was barren. The Lord answered his prayer, and his wife Rebekah became pregnant. The babies jostled each other within her, and she said, 'Why is this happening to me?' So she went to inquire of the Lord.

The prospect of a new baby brings all sorts of hopes and dreams about how things will be during and after the birth. Sometimes it doesn't go according to plan. Perhaps you hoped for a certain kind of delivery and it didn't happen that way. Maybe the routine you have in mind for sleep or for feeding is hard to establish. Maybe health complications have been causing anxiety. Maybe you are short of sleep or simply full of hormones, especially on the infamous 'day three'. And you feel confused, perhaps disappointed.

Rebekah was confused. She hadn't yet given birth, but was uncomfortable, both physically and emotionally. This was a much longed-for pregnancy and an answer to prayer because for a time she had been unable to conceive, so the sense of confusion will have been all the greater. Almost every new parent will at some point ask the question, 'Why is this happening to me?' But if we, like Rebekah, ask God about our situation, he will always answer. He may give us fresh insight into why we are experiencing the problem, or new wisdom to deal with it. He may give us his peace and strength to keep going, or simply his perspective on a situation that we have got out of proportion. If you find yourself confused at what is happening to you today, spend a few moments asking the Lord about it—and then wait. Give him time to answer you and receive comfort from knowing he is in this situation with you.

'Trust in the Lord with all your heart and lean not on your own understanding' (Proverbs 3:5).

THURSDAY

EXODUS 2:1–3

Protectiveness

Now a man of the house of Levi married a Levite woman, and she became pregnant and gave birth to a son. When she saw that he was a fine child, she hid him for three months. But when she could hide him no longer, she got a papyrus basket for him and coated it with tar and pitch. Then she placed the child in it and put it among the reeds along the bank of the Nile.

Pharaoh had decreed that all Israelite baby boys should be killed (Exodus 1:15–22). Fearful that her baby would be killed, this resourceful mother takes action to save her son. It must have taken great courage to do what she did, yet she knew that to do nothing would be even more dangerous.

Which of us, as new parents, cannot relate to this? You might be feeling just now that you could never entrust your baby to someone else to look after, even for an evening, because you feel so protective of him. That will soon pass, and you will come to know the benefits of some time away from your baby to recharge your batteries and be with your partner or your friends. Nevertheless, that protective emotion is God-given. You probably feel you would do anything for him, even to the point of losing your own life.

Moses became one of the significant leaders in biblical history, and God used Moses' parents to help carry out his plan. They had to protect him and then let him go to do what he was made for. God has a plan for your baby too, and you have the joy and responsibility of helping that plan to be carried out. No wonder you feel protective! But God is faithful. You have your part to play, but if you trust him he will work out his purposes for your baby.

'Many are the plans in a human heart, but it is the Lord's purpose that prevails' (Proverbs 19:21).

FRIDAY

LUKE 1:46–49

Joy

And Mary said: 'My soul glorifies the Lord and my spirit rejoices in God my Saviour, for he has been mindful of the humble state of his servant. From now on all generations will call me blessed, for the Mighty One has done great things for me—holy is his name.'

The arrival of a new baby is very exciting, not only for the parents but for those around them as well. It is often the catalyst for the healing of old relationships or the starting of new ones, as there is suddenly a little person to bring new life and joy to both the immediate and the extended family.

The prospect of Mary's baby is no different. As soon as she hears the news, she hurries to visit her cousin Elizabeth, not only to tell about her own baby but also to share in the joy of Elizabeth's pregnancy. Such is the blessing of real community—the ability to share in the highs and lows of the people we live alongside. So Mary breaks into this song of praise to God, expressing her joy at what God has done for her and also the good things he has done for the many others who have trusted him through the generations.

Doubtless the arrival of your little one will have brought you great joy and you may have been overwhelmed at the response of those around you. I remember feeling quite humbled at the delight of others, some of whom were going through hard times themselves, when our first baby was born.

So go ahead and celebrate! This is a wonderful time and a fantastic tribute to an incredible God who loves to give us good gifts. Why not read the passage again, this time using it to express your joy at the way God has blessed you?

'Shout with joy to God, all the earth!' (Psalm 66:1).

WEEKEND ONE

ISAIAH 40:28–31

The Lord's refreshment

Do you not know? Have you not heard? The Lord is the everlasting God, the Creator of the ends of the earth. He will not grow tired or weary, and his understanding no one can fathom. He gives strength to the weary and increases the power of the weak. Even youths grow tired and weary, and young men stumble and fall; but those who hope in the Lord will renew their strength. They will soar on wings like eagles; they will run and not grow weary, they will walk and not be faint.

It's the weekend! I wonder what that means for you? Maybe it means your partner is home and can take the baby for a few hours to enable you to catch up on sleep. Maybe it means your mum or a friend is off work and can come round and give you an extra hand. Or maybe it will simply feel like a continuation of a 'full-on' week.

Whatever your situation, take some time, if you can, to find a place that's comfy and quiet and read the Bible passage to get the gist of it. Then read it again, slowly, allowing the words to sink in. If you get to a phrase that especially strikes you, stay with it and let God speak to you through it as you allow him to lead your thoughts on. Be quiet before God, and invite his Holy Spirit to come and be with you and reveal to you the truth that is to be found in the verses. Then wait. If your baby is still very young and you've been awake a lot in the night, you may fall asleep. Don't worry, make the most of it! But even in our moments of wakeful exhaustion, God will bring rest and refreshment to those who ask him.

Thank you, Father, that you know my every need. Please come now and give me your strength. Enable me, by your Spirit, to accomplish all that I need to do in the next few hours. Amen.

MONDAY

EXODUS 3:10–12a

Fear

'So now, go. I am sending you to Pharaoh to bring my people the Israelites out of Egypt.' But Moses said to God, 'Who am I, that I should go to Pharaoh and bring the Israelites out of Egypt?' And God said, 'I will be with you.'

As time goes on and we get used to the early stages of parenthood, many of the exciting emotions that were so overwhelming at first can become less so, and life begins to settle down.

Don't be surprised if you begin to experience some other feelings, some of which are a bit less welcome. Any parent will tell you that parenthood can bring out in us things we never knew were there—and that we don't like! Moses had been given a task that he felt ill-equipped to do and was feeling insignificant and full of fear, but God reassured him that he was in the right place.

Being a parent can bring a similar feeling. Initially no one expects you to do much other than care for your baby. As you think about doing a bit more, however, you may be panicking, wondering whether you can hold it all together. If you're planning to go back to work eventually, you may be wondering how you'll ever manage it. If you're planning to be at home you may be daunted at being a full-time mum or dad, never having experienced life in your community from Monday to Friday.

Fear can rob us of our confidence that we can be the parent God has called us to be, or that we can still do the job we did before we had our baby, or that we'll eventually get our baby sleeping through the night. There's no need for fear. God has set you the task of raising your baby and he will be with you just as he was with Moses. Take a moment to tell the Lord the things you fear. Then wait and he will fill you with his peace.

'Cast your cares on the Lord and he will sustain you' (Psalm 55:22).

TUESDAY

JOB 6:1–4

Depression

Job replied: 'If only my anguish could be weighed and all my misery be placed on the scales! It would surely outweigh the sand of the seas—no wonder my words have been impetuous. The arrows of the Almighty are in me, my spirit drinks in their poison; God's terrors are marshalled against me.'

Job had been through a severe time of testing in which he lost his family, his possessions and even his health. His friends came to be with him but, however well-intentioned, didn't do much to comfort him. Nevertheless, Job remains faithful to God. Certainly he is miserable and questions why he should experience such disaster, but he is resolved not to turn his back on God and to remain righteous no matter what.

It is not uncommon to go through times of feeling 'low' after having a baby, and some people experience quite severe periods of post-natal depression. Pregnancy and childbirth bring lots of stresses and strains, so it's not surprising that there is sometimes an emotional reaction. You might be tempted to question yourself for feeling down when you have a beautiful baby. Other people, too, might not understand you, if they've never come across it before.

If you do feel like this, talk to someone who can pray with you, support and help you—and tell your health visitor or your GP so that you can get proper medical advice. If it's your wife who's experiencing the 'low', try to be as understanding as you can. With proper support, she will come through it. No one is immune from times of trial, and after having a baby we can be especially vulnerable. But God is mighty and will be with you throughout, even though you may feel quite far from him at times.

'Answer me when I call to you, O my righteous God. Give me relief from my distress; be merciful to me and hear my prayer' (Psalm 4:1).

WEDNESDAY

PSALM 94:1–3

Anger

O Lord, the God who avenges, O God who avenges, shine forth. Rise up, O Judge of the earth; pay back to the proud what they deserve. How long will the wicked, O Lord, how long will the wicked be jubilant?

In these verses we find the psalmist, usually so inclined to humble devotion, launching into an angry outburst against those who are not living a righteous life.

Becoming a parent can be very testing. We can feel stretched to the extreme. With my own children I can experience the whole gamut of emotions in the space of half an hour or less. I remember the first time I felt angry with our first baby who was keeping us up in the night, crying. I was so desperate to sleep and I started to feel weary, then cross, then angry. It took me by surprise. How could I feel such strong negative emotion towards a helpless little baby who, minutes earlier, I had been feeding adoringly? I didn't like what I had become in those few moments of frustration and fatigue.

Anger is a natural and sometimes quite justifiable response, but it's wise to proceed with caution! If you feel this emotion rising up in yourself, it's good to hand the baby to someone else or put her down in her cot. It won't hurt her for a little while. She might even go off to sleep. Go into another room, make a cup of tea and sit down for a few minutes while you calm down. Tell God how you feel and then be still. You will probably feel different very quickly, and then you'll be ready to go back to your baby in a new frame of mind. Sometimes it helps to find a trusted friend with whom you can share these feelings. You could ask them to pray for you to help you deal with the situation that is provoking you.

Lord Jesus, even you were angry at times, but you never responded inappropriately. Please help me as I seek to follow your example.

THURSDAY

PSALM 51:9–12

Guilt

Hide your face from my sins and blot out all my iniquity. Create in me a pure heart, O God, and renew a steadfast spirit within me. Do not cast me from your presence or take your Holy Spirit from me. Restore to me the joy of your salvation and grant me a willing spirit, to sustain me.

The onset of parenthood can sometimes feel like an opportunity to experience more guilt than you've ever done before, and it doesn't go away, even with your second, third or even fourth baby.

David wrote this psalm after he had committed adultery and the prophet Nathan had confronted him with it (2 Samuel 11—12). He is suddenly aware of his terrible sin. David was right to feel guilt. He had sinned, and was full of remorse. These verses show us how desperate he was to be back in right relationship with his God. Most of us have probably known that type of guilt and been glad to know God's forgiveness, like David.

But when we're caring for a new baby, we can often carry unnecessary guilt caused by all manner of things: finding him in the morning with a dirty nappy which he obviously did just before going to sleep, or realizing that his painful wind is due to something you ate last evening, or finding him crying because you left his door open and your toddler has woken him up. Any of these things can leave us feeling mortified.

But these are the kinds of things we'll never get right all the time, so we might as well just relax and stop giving ourselves a hard time. This type of guilt is not from God. He is full of grace and mercy and never intended you to be the perfect parent. In fact, if you get a few things wrong, your baby will grow up without the unrealistic expectation that things will always go his way!

'His compassions… are new every morning' (Lamentations 3:22–23).

FRIDAY

MATTHEW 14:29–31

Failure

'Come,' [Jesus] said. Then Peter got down out of the boat, walked on the water and came toward Jesus. But when he saw the wind, he was afraid and, beginning to sink, cried out, 'Lord, save me!' Immediately Jesus reached out his hand and caught him. 'You of little faith,' he said, 'why did you doubt?'

Peter was so excited at the prospect of walking towards Jesus—and he was full of faith. Everything seemed to be going so well, but then he was overwhelmed by the weather, took his eyes off Jesus and started to sink. However hard he tried not to, he would have felt a failure because of not quite achieving his original goal.

There are moments with a new baby that are similar to Peter's experience. Maybe you expected to breastfeed until your baby was a year old, and after six weeks she isn't gaining weight and you've had to stop. Perhaps others who were in your ante-natal group have their babies sleeping through the night and yours isn't yet. Maybe you put on more weight during your pregnancy than you intended and it isn't shifting. Maybe you're the dad and your wife is feeling down, and nothing you do seems to cheer her up.

This is all so normal! But you don't have to let it get you down. Winston Churchill is reported to have said, 'Success is the ability to move from failure to failure without losing enthusiasm.'

There will be times when, like Peter, you feel you are getting it wrong, but remember: there is always a new day tomorrow. The best thing to do is what Peter did: call out to the Lord. Tell him what you're feeling, then be quiet (try doing it while you're feeding or cuddling your baby) and allow him to speak to you in the silence. I can guarantee he won't tell you you're a failure.

'He will take great delight in you… he will rejoice over you with singing' (Zephaniah 3:17).

ISAIAH 41:10

The Lord's comfort

So do not fear, for I am with you; do not be dismayed, for I am your God. I will strengthen you and help you; I will uphold you with my righteous right hand.

As you reflect back over this last week, you may relate all too easily to some of the emotions we've focused on. You may be feeling somewhat baffled by how you sometimes feel.

As a parent of a brand new baby, you might find yourself putting unrealistic expectations on yourself, especially if you're the one who has given birth and are therefore brimfull with hormones. I remember feeling as if I had become a completely different person overnight as I found myself fretting over details that once I wouldn't even have noticed, or welling up with tears over a news item that, although moving, wouldn't usually cause me to cry.

But just because you've got a new baby, it doesn't mean that anyone expects *you* to be a new and perfect human being, so don't be too hard on yourself. Instead, take a deep breath, read the passage again, and use the words to acknowledge afresh that God is always on hand to help and uphold you in every circumstance. It might help to picture yourself in the arms of God, your Father, and imagine him holding you just as you hold your baby. Think of how you feel about your little one as you comfort him, and remember that God's love for you is even greater than the love you feel for your child. Tell the Lord what you are most troubled by and allow him to take away your fear and restore you again emotionally. You might like to use this prayer to help you.

Thank you, Father, that I can rely on you completely to uphold, comfort and help me. Please do that now. And Lord, I am worried about......... Please help me to trust you for that situation and bring peace into my heart. Amen.

MONDAY

PSALM 139:13–14, 16

Know your value as a person

For you created my inmost being; you knit me together in my mother's womb. I praise you because I am fearfully and wonderfully made; your works are wonderful, I know that full well... All the days ordained for me were written in your book before one of them came to be.

David was full of faith as he wrote these words, trusting in God's truth about himself and praising his creator God for the plan he had had for his life right from day one. How easily do you believe that for yourself?

Caring for a baby is constant feeding, bathing, cleaning up. If you're full-time at home now, you may find that spending so much time in the company of one so tiny leaves you longing for adult company and stimulation. Alone in the house for longer periods of time than you've been used to, while the baby is sleeping or just because you've got nothing planned that day, you may feel rather 'at sea'. You might start to question this massive, overwhelming life-change. Your sense of self-worth and significance might be a bit wobbly, especially if you've given up your career to look after your baby. You may feel a bit insecure and lacking in self-confidence.

But none of these feelings is from God and, if you give him the opportunity and the time, he will demonstrate that to you. Time alone with God is often impossible first thing in the morning when the baby is hungry and the household is getting going, but in the middle of the day there can be space. So why not decide to grasp those times and find a quiet place to sit and be with God. And as you sit in his presence and pour out your heart, he will remind you of the truth about yourself, of how much he loves you and values you for who you are.

'I have loved you with an everlasting love' (Jeremiah 31:3).

TUESDAY

PROVERBS 1:8–9

Know your value as a parent

Listen, my son, to your father's instruction and do not forsake your mother's teaching. They will be a garland to grace your head and a chain to adorn your neck.

Parenthood isn't always rated very highly these days. The world tends to applaud status or salary but not the parent who wants to take family life seriously, simply believing that giving it all they have is very worthwhile and a lot of fun too.

The wisdom of these verses gives a biblical perspective on parenting. The effort that we, as parents, put in to raising our baby will be a blessing to him, causing him to blossom and become the beautiful person God intends him to be. This is the truth. You are performing a very important role. No one's impact on this little person will be greater, certainly in the early years, than yours.

No one else will take as much trouble to shape your child as you will. As you begin to pass on your wisdom to him, and to teach him those all-important qualities of love, patience, kindness, sharing, giving and so on, you will have the joy of developing his little character and seeing him become somebody who makes the world a better place, not only for you but for other people too. Perhaps this will be only in small measure to begin with, but later on who knows who or what he will become?

So acknowledge right at the start how important you are as you raise this gift from God. Allow yourself to ponder for a moment how crucial you are in the life of your baby and to realize that it is no accident that you will be the parent of this child: God has ordained it.

Father, thank you for giving me this child to raise. I pray for him now, that he will grow up to honour me, his parent, and to receive gladly all the positive things that I seek to put into his life. Amen.

WEDNESDAY

MARK 6:30–32

Know the value of other relationships

The apostles gathered around Jesus and reported to him all they had done and taught. Then, because so many people were coming and going that they did not even have a chance to eat, he said to them, 'Come with me by yourselves to a quiet place and get some rest.' So they went away by themselves in a boat to a solitary place.

Jesus had special friends, peer relationships, with whom he could relate at a personal level. And however busy he was, he always made time for his priorities—time with the Father and time with friends. Here we see him deliberately switching off from the demands of work and ministry and trying to get away with the apostles to find refreshment and relaxation.

Initially, with a new baby, it's all-consuming. Other activities go on hold for a few weeks while you get to know your baby and get him through the newborn stage. But once you've surfaced, it will be important to pick up those other relationships again, as well as making new friendships—perhaps through a post-natal group—with other parents who have had a baby at the same time as you.

As your baby grows older, he will be more secure and confident if he knows he's not the centre of your world—a responsibility that would be too much for him to bear. And you will have so much more to give him if you take time out to be stimulated by other people. So invest in your relationships. Take time to talk to your partner every day so that it becomes a habit as your baby grows older. Go out together once a week in the evening. Your baby will feel secure if he sees you enjoying time together. It's healthy for you and for your baby to have some time when you are not together. Then you'll enjoy the time when you are together so much more.

'A friend loves at all times' (Proverbs 17:17).

THURSDAY

2 PETER 3:17–18

Continue to grow spiritually

Therefore, dear friends, since you already know this, be on your guard so that you may not be carried away by the error of lawless men and fall from your secure position. But grow in the grace and knowledge of our Lord and Saviour Jesus Christ. To him be glory both now and forever! Amen.

If you're managing to keep up with these readings, you may not need reminding about growing spiritually! But most people find it harder to keep up a habit of spending time with God in the early days with a new baby. Somehow there is always something to do, and when there isn't, you often find yourself asleep on the sofa.

Peter encourages us in these verses to keep on the right track in our spiritual life. When there is no time to read our Bible and pray, it's easy to become spiritually dry and lose our vitality.

With a new baby to care for and the responsibility of a family, we need more of the grace and knowledge of our Lord and Saviour than ever. You will need God's strength and wisdom to sustain you as you seek to raise your baby. What a blessing to know that you can utterly depend on his resources as you care for your family!

But with your old routine gone and a new, probably much busier one becoming established, you will need to be creative in growing spiritually. Put on a worship CD or a recording of a sermon or Bible reading as you feed your baby. Make sure you get back to church as soon as you can and make use of the crèche if there is one, so that you can have some time to yourself in the service. Talk to the Lord as you walk along with the buggy or stand at the cooker. Don't wait for the return of those blissful stretches of time you may have been used to enjoying—they may not be available for a while. But look for other ways of knowing God's presence, and enjoy the variety!

'Let the word of Christ dwell in you richly' (Colossians 3:16).

FRIDAY

PROVERBS 1:1–5 (ABRIDGED)

Continue to grow as a parent

The proverbs of Solomon… for attaining wisdom and discipline; for understanding words of insight; for acquiring a disciplined and prudent life, doing what is right and just and fair; for giving prudence to the simple, knowledge and discretion to the young—let the wise listen and add to their learning, and let the discerning get guidance.

On the day I gave birth to our first child, I remember lying in my hospital bed looking at her in her little Perspex cot and feeling panic-stricken. I felt clueless about how to care for this little thing I had just brought into the world. Many people had tried to comfort me in my ante-natal anxiety, reassuring me that I would know what to do naturally once the baby was born. And of course that's true to some extent—we do have instincts as parents, which propel us into caring for and protecting our offspring.

But there's lots we can learn. Our reading today underlines the purpose of the Proverbs, and we know how much wisdom is contained in that book. These introductory verses make it clear that a disciplined and prudent life won't just happen; we have to invest in it. They also tell us that it is a good idea to add to our learning and to receive guidance for life. Those of us who are 'simple' and 'young' (v. 4) need the knowledge that godly wisdom offers.

As time went on, I received lots of wisdom from family and friends about how to care for my baby. And even when some of the advice conflicted, I was always glad to hear it, glad to know that there were others who were willing to share their knowledge and experience. I encourage you to do the same. Go on a course, read a book, talk to friends; find out all you can about being a parent.

'Wisdom is supreme; therefore get wisdom. Though it cost all you have, get understanding' (Proverbs 4:7).

WEEKEND THREE

1 CORINTHIANS 6:19–20

The Lord's temple

Do you not know that your body is a temple of the Holy Spirit, who is in you, whom you have received from God? You are not your own; you were bought at a price. Therefore honour God with your body.

We end this section by thinking for a moment about the value of our physical body. At the best of times, we don't always feel great about the way we look. Our society is very image-conscious and we are surrounded in the media by pictures of women, and men, with apparently perfect physiques, skin and hair.

These verses, however, put things into a healthy perspective. They remind us that our bodies are special because they belong to God and the Holy Spirit lives within them. You don't need to buy into the world's insistence on looking immaculate. How much better to concentrate on loving God with your body—eating healthily, getting plenty of sleep (eventually!) and taking exercise.

That said, pregnancy brings with it a dramatic change in body shape and it can take a while to get back to normal after the birth. Some women remain a different shape. And if you have excess weight to lose, it can leave you feeling fairly low in self-esteem and less than eager to get back to physical relations with your partner.

So if you're a mother, take what time you can to look your best. If you can afford it, buy one or two new items of clothing in a style that suits your new shape. If you're a dad, know how important this is for your wife and encourage her in it, perhaps by providing some extra funds to cover the cost. Keep in mind too that your sexual relationship with your partner, though perhaps tricky at first, will be able to resume before too long, as soon as you feel ready.

Thank you, Father, for my body and all that it enables me to do. Help me to take care of myself physically, and please keep me healthy. Amen.

MONDAY

MATTHEW 25:34–36 (ABRIDGED)

Caring physically

Then the King will say… 'Come, you who are blessed by my Father; take your inheritance, the kingdom prepared for you since the creation of the world. For I was hungry and you gave me something to eat, I was thirsty and you gave me something to drink, I was a stranger and you invited me in, I needed clothes and you clothed me, I was sick and you looked after me, I was in prison and you came to visit me.'

Caring for a baby and raising him to become a responsible adult is hard work. It's very rewarding but, like any job, there are aspects of it that can feel mundane and repetitive. So it's good to be reminded that even the most basic tasks associated with caring for your baby are vital. Practical care is life-giving. Without food, a clean nappy and good sleep, your baby will not thrive, and no one is going to attend to these kinds of things like you, his mum or dad.

Here Jesus is saying that to care for the least and the lost is the same as caring for him. Through using this very personal imagery he puts enormous value on people who provide in a practical way for those in need. You are one of those people.

As we do the practical thing for our child, we get into the way of serving. For some, serving is a very natural way of life, but for others it might not have been much of a feature of life before children, so it feels quite new. But with children we have no choice, and it's amazing how we change as we start to care for our baby. Our own needs become less important and the needs of another become all-important. We find ourselves being transformed into the kind of person God wants us all to be—caring and kind to others, doing the work of Jesus in a world that needs it so much.

'Love one another. By this everyone will know that you are my disciples' (John 13:34–35).

TUESDAY

PHILIPPIANS 4:6–7

The power of prayer

Do not be anxious about anything, but in everything, by prayer and petition, with thanksgiving, present your requests to God. And the peace of God, which transcends all understandng, will guard your hearts and your minds in Christ Jesus.

Sometimes the responsibility of being a parent can feel overwhelming. We look at our world and see some of what today's young people get into and we wonder how the future will pan out for our children. It's not just the future, though. Already there will be concerns about whether the baby is feeding and sleeping healthily. Sometimes a child is ill, and that can cause real anxiety. One of my children was rushed to hospital on a few occasions because of a recurring condition, and it was draining.

Here Paul tells us not to be anxious but rather to bring everything to God. By so doing, he says, we will somehow know peace of mind and heart. Many parents today are drawing great comfort from praying for their children who have perhaps taken a wrong turn in life and found themselves in trouble. Often, God in his mercy steps in and acts to turn situations around. It's never too late for God to work a miracle.

You have a brand new baby! You don't need to wait until she grows up before you begin to pray for her. You can pray right now for your child, inviting God into every aspect of her life, asking for protection, wisdom and God's blessing for her. Pray that she'll grow up to make a positive difference in this world. Why not spend a few minutes each evening praying for your baby as you put her to bed? You could use the sample prayer below.

Father, please bless [name]. Please protect her from harm, provide for her needs as she grows, and make her wise in all the choices she makes.

WEDNESDAY

MARK 10:13–16 (ABRIDGED)

Bring your child to Jesus

People were bringing little children to Jesus to have him touch them, but the disciples rebuked them. When Jesus saw this, he was indignant. He said to them, 'Let the little children come to me, and do not hinder them, for the kingdom of God belongs to such as these…' And he took the children in his arms, put his hands on them and blessed them.

I love this little scene, and as I read it I can relate so well to the people who were bringing their children to Jesus. Which of us, knowing the benefits of meeting Jesus, wouldn't have seized the chance of taking our child along to receive all he had to offer?

What strikes me is that, having confronted the disciples who are trying to protect him from hassle, and having taught them an important theological point, he goes on to do so much more than anyone expects. Instead of just touching them, he gathers the children into his arms and blesses them.

Jesus wants to do that for your baby. He wants to bless her beyond anything you can imagine. He has wonderful plans for her life which he longs to see fulfilled, and they will be—if only you will bring your child to Jesus. It's never too soon to start. We've talked already about praying for your baby, but you can do other things: read Bible stories together as soon as she is able to look at the pictures, sing or play recordings of praise songs, teach her to pray, take her to church so that she can feel at home there and eventually learn to worship for herself. Babies take in far more than we realize, and every effort you make to introduce your little one to spiritual things will make a difference.

'See that you do not look down on one of these little ones. For I tell you that their angels in heaven always see the face of my Father in heaven' (Matthew 18:10).

DEUTERONOMY 11:18–19

Teach your child how to live

Fix these words of mine in your hearts and minds; tie them as symbols on your hands and bind them on your foreheads. Teach them to your children, talking about them when you sit at home and when you walk along the road, when you lie down and when you get up.

As your baby grows a little older and goes to nursery and school, he will begin to hear all sorts of things about all sorts of subjects. He will hear things you'd probably rather he didn't hear, and things that conflict with your family's way of thinking.

In our Bible passage, the Israelites are being urged not only to live out the instructions God is giving them themselves, but also to pass them on to their children. Why? Because to obey the Lord's commands will give them every opportunity of a long life in the land of blessing.

We can learn from this. We too need to take every opportunity to pass on to our child, once he is old enough to understand, the lessons we believe to be important for life. We will teach him about following God's guidelines, making it known that to remain within those will bring safety and blessing for our child.

I try constantly to talk to my children about what is important to me: that a relationship with God is important, that commitment to people is important, that being able to laugh at yourself with others is helpful, that trying your best is important, that helping and being kind to other people is important and brings satisfaction. Your baby will need you to talk to him about what is important to you. If you start while he's small, he will have every opportunity of taking it all on board for himself.

'The statutes of the Lord are trustworthy, making wise the simple' (Psalm 19:7a).

PSALM 78:4b–7

Teach all you know about God

We will tell the next generation the praiseworthy deeds of the Lord, his power, and the wonders he has done. He decreed statutes for Jacob and established the law in Israel, which he commanded our forefathers to teach their children, so the next generation would know them, even the children yet to be born, and they in turn would tell their children. Then they would put their trust in God and would not forget his deeds but would keep his commands.

What an opportunity we have as parents to bring up our child to be familiar with and to be part of the story of God!

These verses record the psalmist's resolve to tell of the goodness of God and his guidelines to the next generation, so that they in turn can pass the knowledge to their children and benefit from the security of a life of trust in him.

In those days, word of mouth would have been the only means of passing things on. While today's means of communication are far more sophisticated, there is a lot to be said for conversation and for repeating truths again and again so that they become very much part of our children's lives.

As I write, I am in hospital with my youngest child, who has a broken arm and needed surgery. In the rush to pack, we forgot his Bible, so at bedtime I offered to tell him a Bible story. He had a better idea. He told me a family favourite—the one of the Israelites escaping through the Red Sea. We talked together about how 'clever' God is and how powerful.

I want to tell my children as much as I can about God while they are with me. You can do that too. It's the best gift you can give them.

Father, give me wisdom as I teach [name] all I know about you. Amen.

ISAIAH 54:13

The Lord's promises

All your sons will be taught by the Lord, and great will be your children's peace.

If you've made it to the end of this booklet and your baby is still small, you deserve a medal. But I hope that, as you've made your way through these readings, you have found encouragement and refreshment in them. Our concluding verse reminds us that not only are we doing our utmost to raise our children responsibly, but the Lord too wants to nurture and guide them. If that happens, our children, it says, will live in peace. How comforting those words will be when you find yourself dealing with a toddler or teenage tantrum in the years to come!

But we know that the peace the Lord offers runs far deeper than sorting out a tantrum. It is the peace that comes from knowing that we are living within the safety of his guidelines, seeking to bless other people and do good as far as we are able. This is the kind of peace that our children will ultimately experience if we expose them to the Lord's teaching. And nothing we ourselves can offer or do for our children can ever compare with what God can offer them through a relationship with him.

As a parent, we will never get everything right, but our mistakes keep us humble and help us learn how to do better next time. As we entrust our own and our children's lives to God, he will always be alongside us, giving us wisdom, help, strength and peace if we call on him. My prayer is that you might know every one of these blessings in this exciting and challenging season of family life.

Thank you, Lord, that as I raise my baby, I don't have to rely on my own strength because you, the perfect Father, are always there to help me. I commit [name] to you again today and ask that he/she will grow up to honour you and to know the blessing of a relationship with you. Amen.

Bible reading notes from BRF

If you have found this booklet helpful and would like to continue reading the Bible regularly, you may like to explore BRF's three series of Bible reading notes.

NEW DAYLIGHT

New Daylight offers a devotional approach to reading the Bible. Each issue covers four months of daily Bible readings and reflection from a regular team of contributors, who represent a stimulating mix of church backgrounds. Each day's reading provides a Bible passage (text included), comment and prayer or thought for reflection. In *New Daylight* the Sundays and special festivals from the church calendar are noted on the relevant days, to help you appreciate the riches of the Christian year.

DAY BY DAY WITH GOD

Day by Day with God (published jointly with Christina Press) is written especially for women, with a regular team of contributors. Each four-monthly issue offers daily Bible readings, with key verses printed out, helpful comment, a prayer or reflection for the day ahead, and suggestions for further reading.

GUIDELINES

Guidelines is a unique Bible reading resource that offers four months of in-depth study written by leading scholars. Contributors are drawn from around the world, as well as the UK, and they represent a thought-provoking breadth of Christian tradition. *Guidelines* is written in weekly units consisting of six sections plus an introduction and a final section of points for thought and prayer.

If you would like to subscribe to one or more of these sets of Bible reading notes, please use the order form overleaf.

NOTES SUBSCRIPTIONS

❑ I would like to give a gift subscription (please complete both name and address sections below)

❑ I would like to take out a subscription myself (complete name and address details only once)

This completed coupon should be sent with appropriate payment to BRF. Alternatively, please write to us quoting your name, address, the subscription you would like for either yourself or a friend (with their name and address), the start date and credit card number, expiry date and signature if paying by credit card.

Gift subscription name ______________________

Gift subscription address ______________________

____

______________________ Postcode __________

Please send beginning with the January / May / September issue: (delete as applicable)

(please tick box)	UK	SURFACE	AIR MAIL
NEW DAYLIGHT	❑ £12.00	❑ £13.35	❑ £15.60
GUIDELINES	❑ £12.00	❑ £13.35	❑ £15.60
DAY BY DAY WITH GOD	❑ £12.75	❑ £14.10	❑ £16.35

Please complete the payment details below and send your coupon, with appropriate payment to: **BRF, First Floor, Elsfield Hall, 15–17 Elsfield Way, Oxford OX2 8FG.**

Your name ______________________

Your address ______________________

____

______________________ Postcode __________

Total enclosed £ __________ (cheques made payable to 'BRF')

Payment: cheque ❑ postal order ❑ Visa ❑ Mastercard ❑ Switch ❑

Card number: ☐☐☐☐☐☐☐☐☐☐☐☐☐☐☐☐☐☐☐

Expiry date of card: ☐☐☐☐ Issue number (Switch): ☐☐☐☐

____

Signature (essential if paying by credit/Switch card)

❑ Please do not send me further information about BRF publications.

BRF resources are available from your local Christian bookshop. BRF is a Registered Charity

Christian bookshops: All Christian bookshops stock BRF publications.
Telephone: To place your order, dial 01865 319700.
Fax: To place your order, dial 01865 319701.
Web: To place your order using the BRF website, visit www.brf.org.uk

REF	TITLE	PRICE	QTY	TOTAL
1 84101 418 4	Bible Readings for Special Times: Bereavement	£1.99		
1 84101 494 X	Bible Readings for Special Times: Confirmation	£1.99		
1 84101 447 8	Bible Readings for Special Times: Going to College	£1.99		
1 84101 421 4	Bible Readings for Special Times: Ill Health	£1.99		
1 84101 427 3	Bible Readings for Special Times: Marriage	£1.99		
1 84101 457 5	Bible Readings for Special Times: Moving House	£1.99		
1 84101 487 7	Bible Readings for Special Times: New Baby	£1.99		
1 84101 430 3	Bible Readings for Special Times: Retirement	£1.99		

POSTAGE & PACKING CHARGES				
Order value	UK	Europe	Surface	Air Mail
Under £7.00	£1.25	£3.00	£3.50	£5.50
£7.01–£29.99	£2.25	£5.50	£6.50	£10.00
Over £30.00	FREE	Prices on request		

Total Value of books	
Postage	
TOTAL	

Name ______________________________

Account Number (if known) ______________________________

Address ______________________________

____

______________________________ Postcode ______________

Telephone ______________ Email ______________________________

❒ Please email me with information about BRF resources and services

Method of payment:

❑ Cheque ❑ Mastercard ❑ Visa ❑ Postal Order ❑ Maestro

Card no.

Issue no. of Switch card Expires

Shaded boxes for Maestro use only

Signature ______________________________

Date ___ / ___ / ___

All orders must be accompanied by the appropriate payment. Please make cheques payable to BRF.

Please send your completed form to:

brf, First Floor, Elsfield Hall,
15–17 Elsfield Way,
Oxford OX2 8FG

PROMO REF: BRST-NB

brf is a Registered Charity